FOOD

Chris Deshpande

Photographs by Zul Mukhida

Contents

A&C Black · London

About this book

Did you know that some of the dyes we use to colour fabric come from vegetables and spices? This book is about food and cooking from around the world. It shows you how to make craft objects based on food and gives you plenty of ideas to help you design your own.

In this book you can find out about customs, crafts and traditions based on food. At the back of the book, there is information on how to find out more about these crafts and traditions, with details about places to visit and books to read.

Some of the craft activities in this book are more complicated than others and will take longer to finish. It might be fun to ask some friends to help with these activities, such as making salt dough beads on page 6.

Before you start working on any of the craft projects, read through the instructions carefully. Each step-by-step instruction has a number. Look for the same number in the picture to see how to make each stage of your model.

Before you begin

Collect together everything listed in the 'you will need box'.

Ask an adult's permission if you are going to use a sharp tool, dye cloth or use an oven.

Prepare a clear work surface.

If the activity is going to be messy, cover the surface with old newspaper or a waterproof sheet.

3

Pretzels

Pretzels are a kind of hard bread baked in knot shapes with a salty coating. They come from Germany where they were traditionally eaten at carnival time. Now they are eaten all year round as snacks. Many people think they were first made by a baker who was imprisoned for selling bad bread. He was told that he could go free if he baked something that let the sun shine through it three times. He baked pretzels.

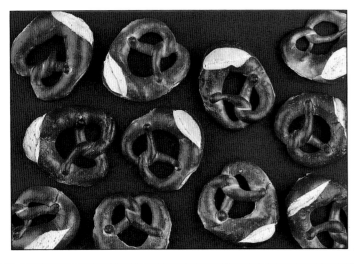

Try making some pretzels

You will need: a small saucepan, 2 small bowls, a mixing bowl, a measuring jug, a sieve, a fork, a clean cloth, a baking tray, a pastry brush, a spoon, a cooker; ¼ teaspoon dried yeast, ¼ teaspoon cinnamon powder, 25g sugar, 50g butter, 125ml milk, 1 egg, 275g plain flour, pinch of salt and sea salt if possible.

1 **Ask an adult to help you make the pretzels.** Wash your hands. Heat the milk in the saucepan until it is just lukewarm. Pour the milk into a small bowl and stir in the dried yeast and sugar. Leave the mixture in a warm place for about 10 minutes until it's frothy. Wash the saucepan.

2 Sift the flour, cinnamon and salt into the mixing bowl. Make a well in the middle and pour in the yeast mixture.

3 Break the egg into a bowl and beat it with a fork. Save some of the egg for later. Gently heat the butter in a saucepan until it is runny. Pour the butter and egg into the flour mixture.

4 Mix it together with your hands. Sprinkle some flour on to a clean kitchen surface and fold and press, or knead, the dough for about 5 minutes. Cover the dough with the cloth and leave it to rise for about 20 minutes.

5 Divide the dough into small balls and roll them into long sausage shapes. Can you make shapes which will let the sun shine through three times? Put the pretzels on the baking tray. Leave them to rise in a warm place for 20 minutes. Set the oven to 220°C, 425°F, Gas mark 7.

Brush the pretzels with beaten egg and sprinkle with sea salt. Bake them in the oven for 10 minutes until they are brown.

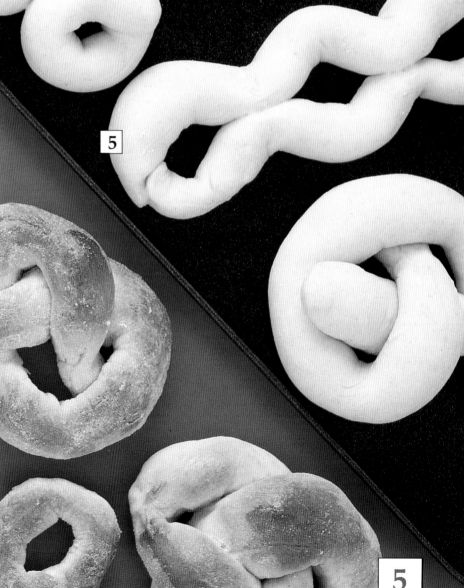

Salt dough beads

Dough is something we usually think of as food. Bread, pastry and biscuits are made from dough, but salt dough is not meant to be eaten. It can be used to make models, beads and other jewellery.

Try making some salt dough jewellery. Before you begin, look at the shape and colours of different kinds of beads and pendants to get some ideas for your own designs.

You will need: 200g flour, 2 tablespoons salt, water, a mixing bowl, a darning needle, a baking tray, paintbrushes, paints, cord or thick thread or shirring elastic, an oven set at Gas mark 2 (150°C, 300°F).

1 Put the flour and salt in a bowl. Add a little bit of water, stir the mixture and add some more water until you have a stiff dough. Fold and press, or knead, the dough for about five minutes.

2 Break off a small piece of dough and roll or press it into the size and shape bead you want. Push a thick darning needle through the centre of the bead. Make many more beads in this way. Experiment making different sized and shaped beads.

3 Place the beads on the tray and **ask an adult to put it in the oven** for about an hour.

4 When the beads are cool, paint them. Thread the needle with cord and tie a knot at the end. Thread your beads on to the cord. Tie the ends of the cord together.

You could make an interesting shape from salt dough for a pendant. Or try threading small beads on to shirring elastic to make a hair tie or bracelet.

4

Milk painting

In the seventeenth century, many Europeans travelled to North America to settle. Often, they travelled thousands of miles before reaching their final destination and carried very little with them. When the settlers arrived, they made furniture and household utensils from wood which they cut down themselves. Sometimes they decorated the wood with a special kind of paint made from milk, and fruit and vegetables dyes. This milk paint dried to a very hard finish. Some of this milk-painted furniture has lasted for over three hundred years.

Try decorating a wooden fruit crate with milk paint

You will need: a bowl, a tablespoon, dried non-fat milk powder, warm water, natural food colouring including turmeric, paint brushes, varnish, an old wooden fruit crate from a supermarket or greengrocer's, sandpaper, a hammer.

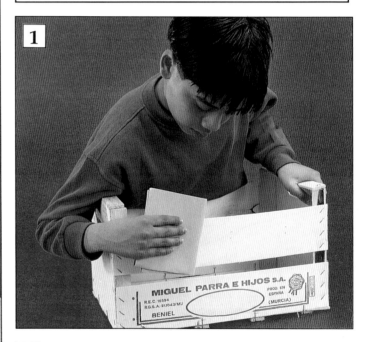

1 Smooth the rough surfaces of the crate with sandpaper. Hammer in any nails which stick out.

2 Put about two tablespoons of milk powder into the bowl. Add small amounts of water until you make a thick smooth paste. Add a few drops of food colouring or half a teaspoon of turmeric to the mixture. You can make different shades of colour by using different amounts of food colouring.

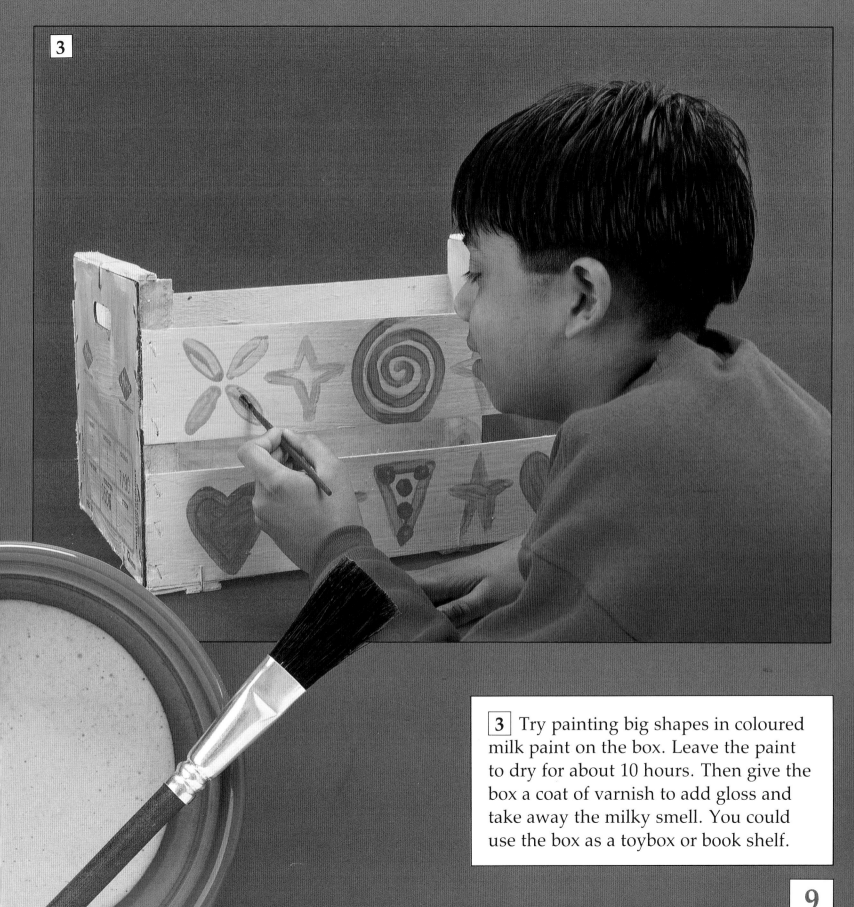

3 Try painting big shapes in coloured milk paint on the box. Leave the paint to dry for about 10 hours. Then give the box a coat of varnish to add gloss and take away the milky smell. You could use the box as a toybox or book shelf.

Natural dyes

Some colours have special meanings. In ancient Rome, only the caesars could wear purple, a colour which came from an expensive dye made from shellfish. And traditionally the robes of Buddhist monks were dyed yellow with saffron which comes from crocuses.

For thousands of years, people have experimented with dyes to colour their clothes. Dyes can be made from fruit and vegetables, berries, herbs, flowers, twigs and bark, and also from some animals.

Ask an adult to help you dye an old pair of cotton socks or a vest with beetroot, red cabbage or turmeric. The dye will take best on white cotton material. And remember always to wash your dyed clothes separately in case the dye runs.

> **You will need: a sharp knife, a chopping board, one saucepan which isn't enamel, water, salt, rubber gloves, a sieve, a pair of old cotton socks or a vest. One of the following: two teaspoons of turmeric, half a large red cabbage or one large uncooked beetroot.**

1 Put the washed beetroot in the saucepan with 1 litre of water. Bring the water to the boil and simmer for about 30 minutes. Take the beetroot out of the saucepan. You can peel the beetroot and eat it in salads.

Carefully sieve the beetroot water into a bowl. Stir 4 tablespoons of salt into the water. Put the socks and water back into the saucepan. Simmer for about 20 minutes.

When the saucepan is cool, put it in the sink. Wear rubber gloves and rinse the socks in cold water. Hang them up to dry.

2 Try dyeing a pair of socks with red cabbage. Slice up the cabbage, then follow the instructions for dyeing with beetroot, but use cabbage water instead.

3 Put 2 teaspoons of turmeric into a saucepan with 1 litre of cold water. Bring the water to the boil. Stir about 4 tablespoons of salt into the water. Add the socks and put the saucepan back on the stove. Simmer for about 20 minutes. When the saucepan is cool put it in the sink. Wear rubber gloves and rinse the socks in cold water. Hang them up to dry.

Flour and water paste batik

Batik is a way of decorating fabric. A design is painted on to the fabric with hot wax and then the fabric is dyed. The fabric does not take the dye where it is covered by the wax design. When the wax is removed, the design shows up clearly.

The art of batik started in China and then became popular in India and the Far East. This picture shows a man removing a hot wax batik design from fabric with an iron.

Hot wax batik can be dangerous, but you can achieve nearly the same effect with flour and water paste. Try decorating a handkerchief with a batik design. It's best to use a white cotton handkerchief.

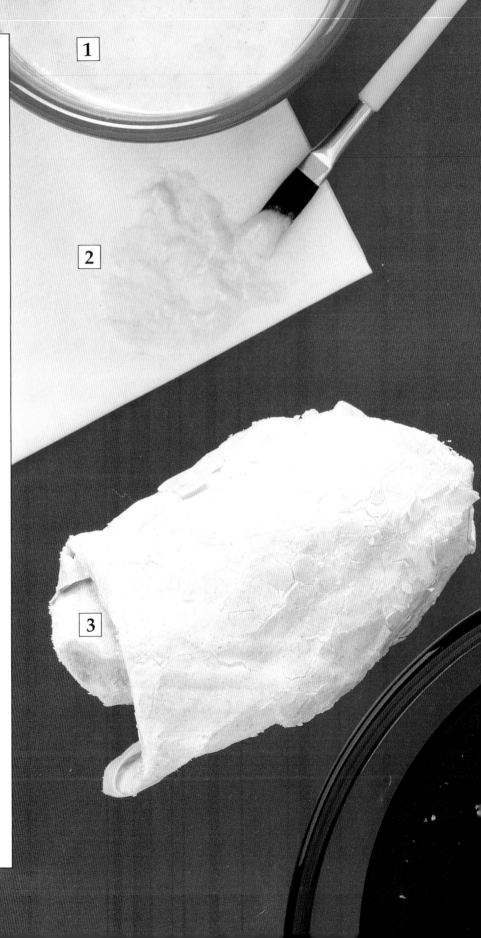

You will need: a mixing bowl, flour and water, a white cotton handkerchief, a thick paintbrush, a bucket, rubber gloves, cold water dye, a knife, a tablespoon.

1 Mix 4 tablespoons of flour with 3 tablespoons of water to make a smooth paste.

2 Use a paintbrush to paint a thick layer of paste all over the handkerchief on both sides. Leave the paste to dry overnight.

3 When the handkerchief is dry, scrunch it up so that the paste cracks and looks like dry earth.

4 **Ask an adult to help you make the cold water dye in a bowl.** Follow the instructions on the packet carefully and wear rubber gloves. Soak the handkerchief in the dye for about one hour. Then take it out and rinse it thoroughly in cold water. Hang it up to dry.

5 When the handkerchief is dry, use a knife to scrape away any paste which is left. Rinse the handkerchief again, then wash it in soapy water and leave to dry. Always wash your dyed handkerchief separately in case the dye runs.

Try making some different batik patterns. You could paint paste circles on to a handkerchief and then dye it.

5

Potato prints

In the 1920s, potato printing was made popular by a teacher in France. She called the craft PDT which are the first letters of the French word for potato, 'pomme de terre'.

You can make complicated looking patterns from simple potato prints. Many patterns are based on squares, circles or triangles. Try making a printed pattern with a potato.

> **You will need: paper and pencil, scissors, a large potato, 3 dressmaking pins, a large sharp knife, a small sharp knife, poster paints or thick powder paint mixture, a paintbrush, paper for printing on.**

1 Cut out a simple shape in paper which will fit on to half a cut potato. Cut a pattern into your paper shape. Think about how you can repeat this shape to make a pattern.

2 **Ask an adult to help you cut the potato in half with the large knife.**

3 Pin the shape to the cut surface of one half of the potato. **Ask an adult to help you cut away the potato around the shape.** Take the paper shape and pins off the potato.

4 Brush paint on to the raised part of the potato and press it on to the paper. Here are a few suggestions for ways to make patterns. Try out your own ideas as well.

5 Repeat a print in straight rows.

6 Print in rotation, which means moving the potato print round each time like a wheel.

7 Try using two stamps to make a printed pattern.

8 Try printing a picture. To make a flower, use one stamp for the leaves, one for the stem and another for the petals.

Try making your own gift-wrapping paper or greetings cards. If you make a small design, you could print a border for writing paper.

Seed necklaces

For centuries, all over the world, beads have been used to make jewellery and decorate clothes and items around the house. Native Americans sew beads on to their clothes and moccasin shoes. And in Victorian England beads were used to decorate teapot stands and fire screens.

Beads are made from precious gems, shells, wood, clay, glass, nuts, berries, stones and seeds.

Try making a melon seed necklace

You will need: melon seeds from about four honeydew melons, washing up liquid and water, absorbent paper, cotton sewing thread, a darning needle, scissors.

1 Wash the melon seeds in soapy water. Rinse them and leave them to dry on absorbent paper for about two days.

2 Drape some cotton around your neck and decide how long you want your necklace to be. Measure half as much again. Cut three pieces of cotton to this length. Tie them together at one end. Thread all three lengths of cotton through the darning needle.

3 Push the needle through about fifteen melon seeds and slide them down to the knot.

4 Pull out two of the strands of cotton from the eye of the needle. Thread about fifteen seeds on to the first strand of cotton which is still in the needle.

5 Pull out the first strand from the needle and thread the needle with the second strand. Push about fifteen seeds on to this strand.

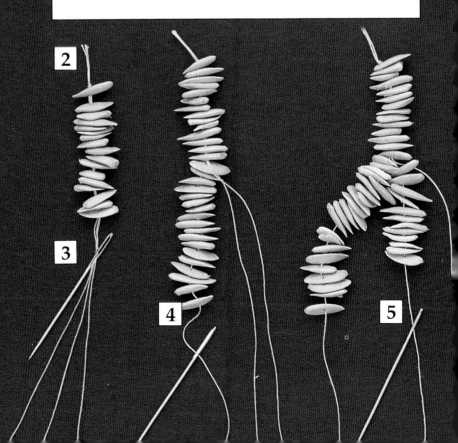

6 Pull out the second strand, thread the needle with the third strand and push about fifteen seeds on to it.

7 Thread all three strands back through the needle and push on about fifteen melon seeds.

8 Now thread the first strand through the needle and repeat the steps as before. Continue threading the seeds in this way until the necklace is the length you want it. To finish, all three strands should be pushed through some melon seeds. Then tie the cotton strands at each end of the necklace together.

Try making necklaces from single strands of seeds which are twisted together.

If you cannot collect enough seeds for a necklace, you could make a bracelet from the seeds from one melon. Use shirring elastic instead of cotton thread.

Appliqué fruit bag

Appliqué is one of the oldest known types of embroidery, where fabric shapes are sewn on to material to make a collage. It's thought to have been invented by the ancient Chinese who wanted to patch up holes in worn-out clothes.

This appliquéd wall-hanging comes from Mexico.

Try making a bag decorated with appliquéd fruit shapes

You will need: a pencil and paper, a rectangle of backing cloth which won't fray approximately 28 × 46cm, chalk, different coloured felts, pins, a needle, cotton and embroidery thread, scissors, a length of cord approximately 1m, a safety pin.

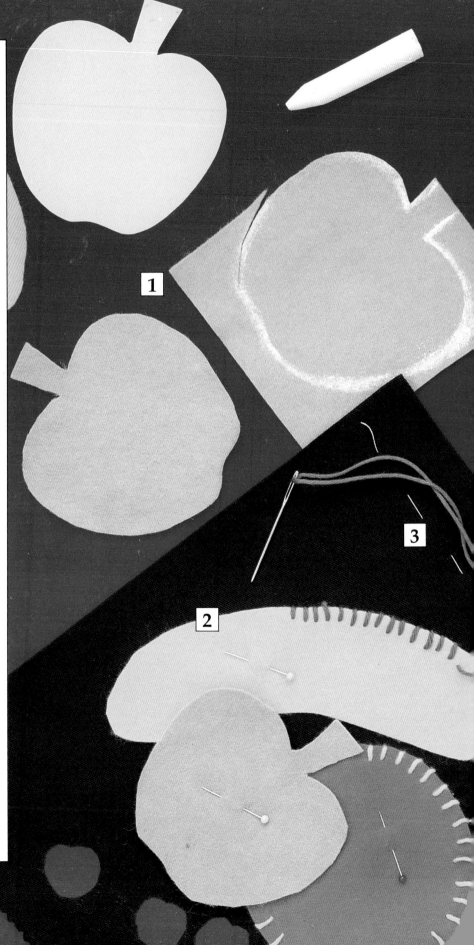

1 Fold the backing cloth in half. Think about your fruit design which will fit on half the cloth. Sketch a couple of fruits on paper first so that you get an idea of the size of the shapes you need.

Chalk fruit shapes on to the back of the felts. Cut out the shapes. Turn them over so you can't see any chalk marks.

2 Arrange the fruit shapes on the cloth so that some of the shapes overlap each other. Pin or make a loose stitch in the middle of each shape.

3 Start with a shape at the top and sew around only the edge of the shape that you can see, as shown. Then move to another shape, again sewing around only the edge that you can see. Sew all the shapes to the cloth in this way.

4 To make the picture into a bag, turn the cloth picture-side down. Fold the top of the cloth over towards you by about 4 centimetres and pin or tack in place. Stitch along the edge with small close stitches.

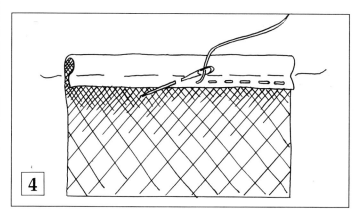

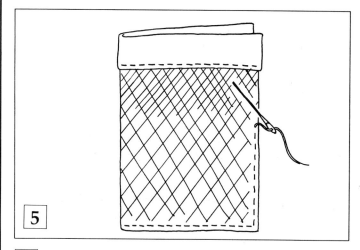

5 Fold the backing cloth in half, so that the picture is inside. Stitch the bottom edges together, then stitch the side edges together. Leave the openings in the top free.

6 Turn the bag the right way out. Fasten one end of the cord to the safety pin. Push it into one of the openings in the top hem. Push it through until it comes out the other end. Sew or tie the ends of the cord together.

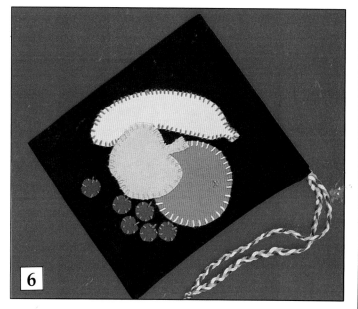

Musical instruments

Often, musical instruments are made out of fruit and seeds. In many parts of Africa, dried gourds, which are fruits, are made into shakers and maracas. In the Caribbean, coconut shells are used to make musical instruments called guiros. The outside of the coconut shell is cut with grooves, then a stick is scraped across the ridges in time to the beat of the music.

In South America, a musical instrument called a rainmaker is made from a hollow bamboo cane with sticks pushed through it. Dried corn is put in the cane which is then sealed at both ends. Then the ends of the sticks are cut off. When the cane is turned upside down, the corn falls all the way down the tube, tumbling over the sticks, making a sound like rain.

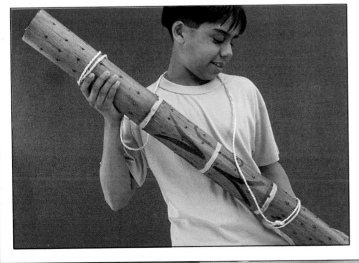

Try making your own rainmaker

You will need: a cardboard tube with a lid for each end (or lids made from cardboard and sticky tape), about 40 lolly sticks, sharp scissors, a handful of dried chickpeas, paintbrushes and paints.

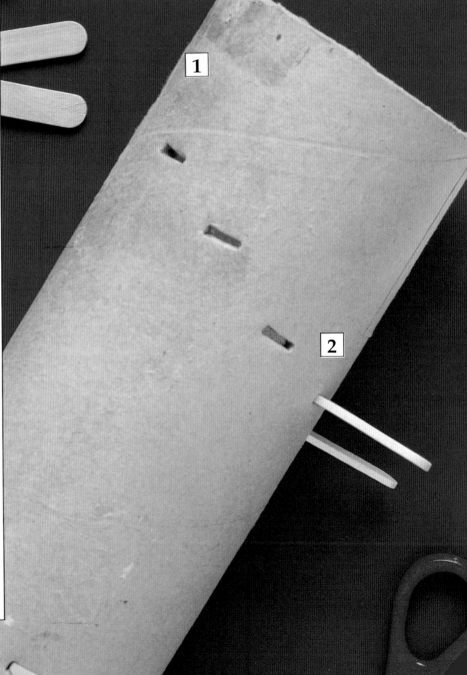

1

2

1 **Ask an adult to help you make slits in the tube.** Hold the scissors with the blades together, pointed away from your body, and make a slit in the tube. A lolly stick should fit tightly in the slit. Make a spiral pattern of slits in the tube.

2 Push a lolly stick into the first slit until it touches the other side of the tube. Put a lolly stick into each slit.

3 Put one lid on one end of the tube or cover with a cardboard circle and sticky tape. Place a big handful of dried chickpeas into the tube. Put the other lid on the other end of the tube or seal it with cardboard and sticky tape.

4 Paint and decorate your rainmaker.

Turn your rainmaker upside down and listen to the sound it makes. Try making a rainmaker with a different sized tube and a different amount of chickpeas. Can you make the sound of heavy rain or a light shower?

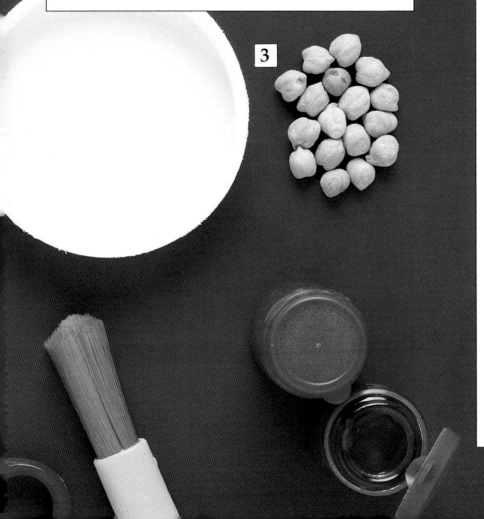

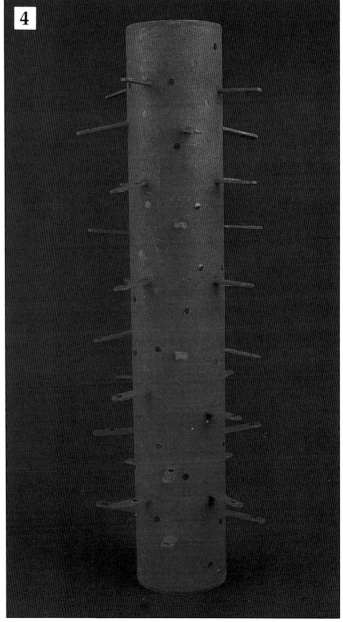

21

Rangoli patterns

Rangoli patterns are made from coloured flour paste, rice and spices. They are a traditional way of decorating Hindu homes for celebrations and festivals.

During the Diwali festival, rangoli patterns are made at the entrance to homes to welcome the Goddess Lakshmi, who is said to bring health and happiness. At weddings, rangoli patterns often decorate the place where the bride and groom sit. Traditional rangoli floor designs are usually based on the lotus flower and the mango leaf.

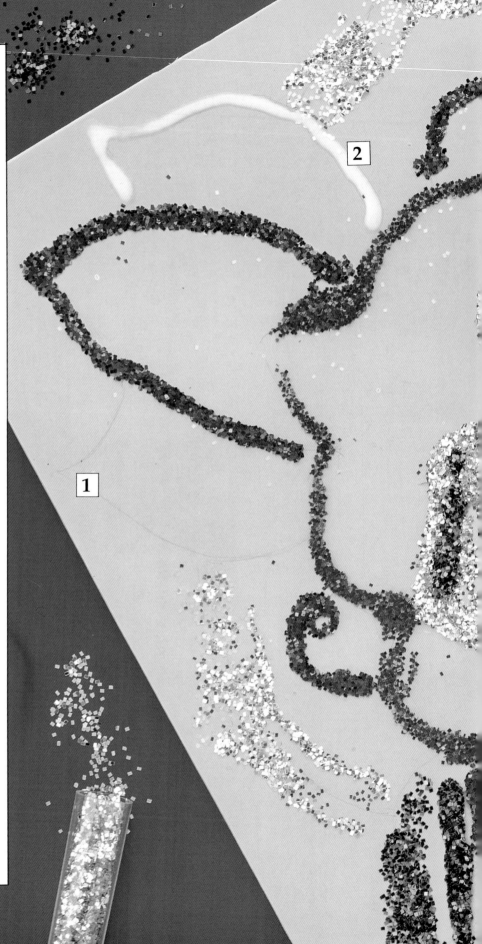

Try making a rangoli pattern with glitter

You will need: paper, PVA glue, a pencil, different coloured glitter, a paintbrush, lots of newspaper.

1 This activity can be messy, so before you begin put lots of old newspapers down on your work surface. On a piece of paper, draw your design in pencil. It's best to start with a simple design.

2 Carefully paint or squeeze a thin line of glue over part of the pencil design.

3 Hold the tube of glitter and pour it over the line of glue. Carefully tip up your glitter design on to another piece of paper and shake off any spare glitter. Make a small paper funnel and pour the spare glitter back into the tube. Continue applying different coloured glitters to your pattern in this way.

3

A Mexican pinata

A pinata is a Mexican papier-mâché toy which is filled with sweets, fruit, nuts and small presents. But unusually it is a toy which is meant to be broken, especially at parties and Christmas time. Sometimes pinatas are made in the shape of animals and cartoon characters. They are hung from branches and posts. Everyone sings a song, while one blindfolded child tries to hit the pinata with a big stick. When the pinata breaks, everyone tries to catch the sweets and nuts which fall to the ground.

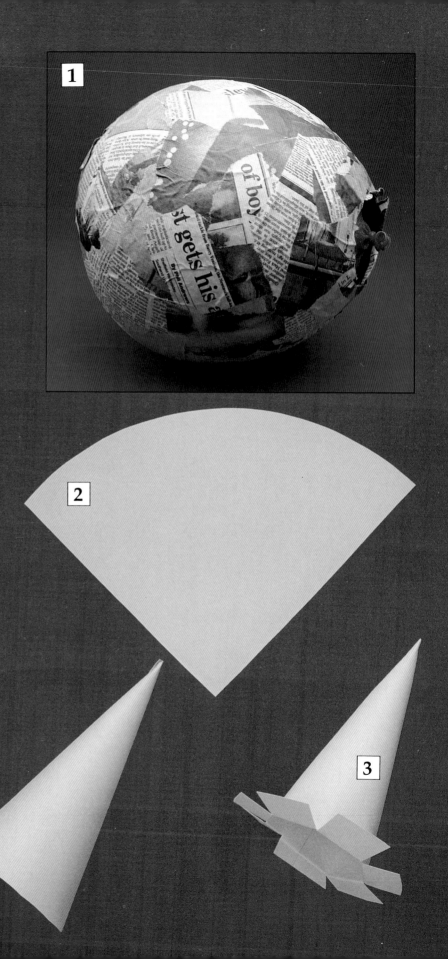

Try making a pinata for a party

You will need: a large balloon, newspaper torn into strips, a small bowl of wallpaper paste without fungicide, a thick brush, a pair of compasses, scissors, sticky tape, paints and paintbrushes, sweets, nuts and small presents to put inside.

1 Blow up the balloon and tie the end. Dip a piece of newspaper into the paste and then place it on the balloon. Cover the ballon with pasted paper, overlapping the pieces slightly to make a smooth surface. At the end of the balloon, near the tie, leave a circle uncovered with a diameter of approximately 8 centimetres. Cover the balloon with about four layers of paper. When the papier-mâché is dry, burst the balloon.

2 Cut out a cardboard quarter-circle with a radius of about 24 centimetres. Make the quarter-circle into a cone shape and glue the sides together. Make more cones in this way. One of your cones must be big enough to cover the hole in the papier-mâché balloon.

3 Make small cuts around the base of the cones and fold up the flaps.

4

4 Glue and then papier-mâché the cones to the balloon. Fill the pinata with your sweets, nuts and toys. Then seal the hole in the end of the balloon with the last cone. Paint and decorate your pinata.

Hansel and Gretel

Food plays an important part in stories from around the world. In the story of Hansel and Gretel, two children are lost in the woods when they suddenly come across a house made of gingerbread.

Try making a gingerbread house. If you get together with friends, you could make a gingerbread village. First you need to make the gingerbread biscuit shapes. Ask an adult to help you make the biscuits. The next pages show you how to make the biscuits into houses.

You will need: a pencil and paper, scissors; a mixing bowl, a small bowl, a wooden spoon, a sieve, a rolling pin, a knife, a pastry brush, a greased baking tray, oven gloves, a wire rack; 225g plain flour, 100g margarine, 100g soft brown sugar, 2 teaspoons ground ginger, 1 teaspoon mixed spice, 1 egg, 3 teaspoons of honey, an oven set to Gas mark 6 (200°C, 410°F).

1 To make a simple house, you will need to cut out in paper two of each of the shapes shown here.

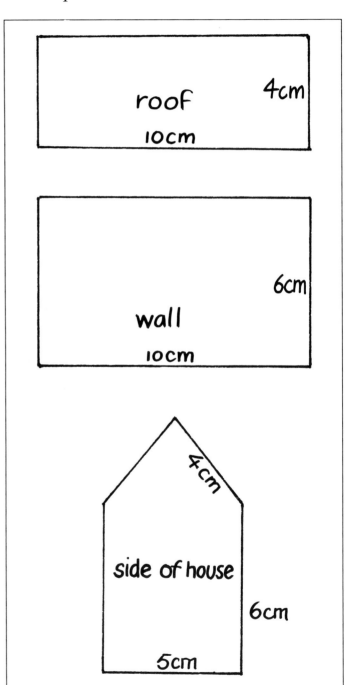

roof   4cm
10cm

wall   6cm
10cm

side of house   4cm
6cm
5cm

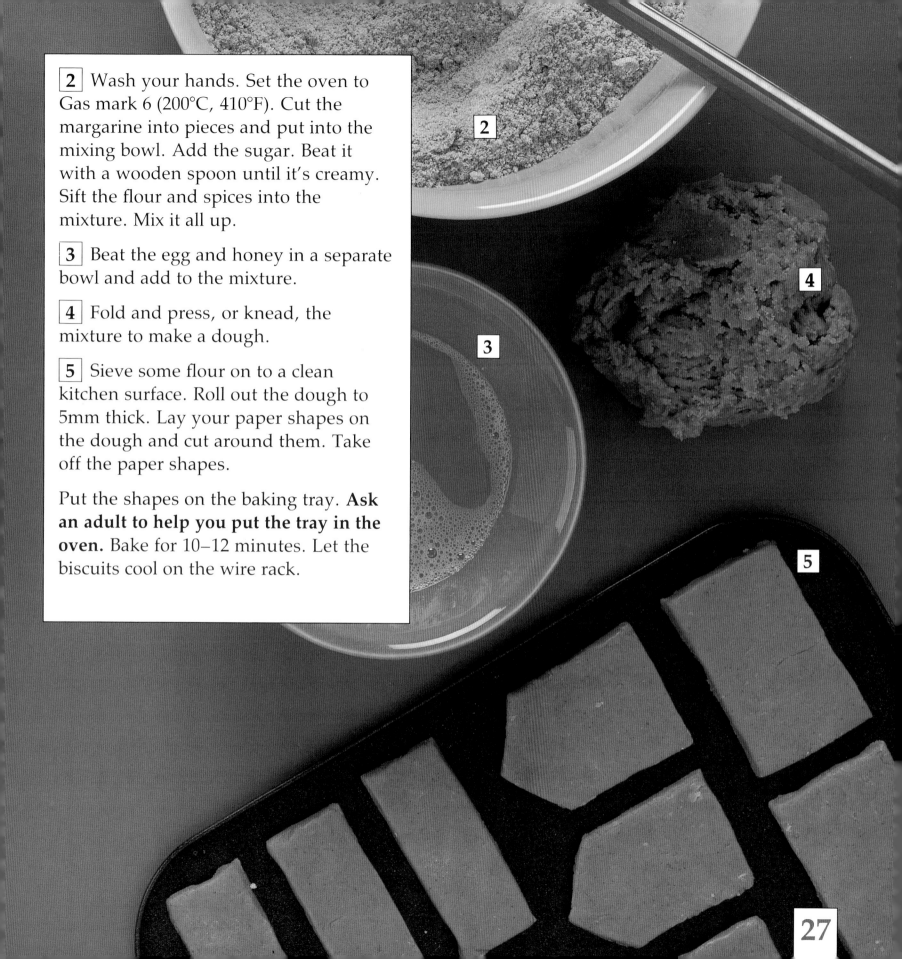

2 Wash your hands. Set the oven to Gas mark 6 (200°C, 410°F). Cut the margarine into pieces and put into the mixing bowl. Add the sugar. Beat it with a wooden spoon until it's creamy. Sift the flour and spices into the mixture. Mix it all up.

3 Beat the egg and honey in a separate bowl and add to the mixture.

4 Fold and press, or knead, the mixture to make a dough.

5 Sieve some flour on to a clean kitchen surface. Roll out the dough to 5mm thick. Lay your paper shapes on the dough and cut around them. Take off the paper shapes.

Put the shapes on the baking tray. **Ask an adult to help you put the tray in the oven.** Bake for 10–12 minutes. Let the biscuits cool on the wire rack.

A gingerbread village

You will need: a mixing bowl, a wooden spoon, icing sugar, water, a teaspoon, marzipan, a pastry brush; dried fruit and sweets for decoration.

1 Add a little bit of water to the icing sugar to make a thick paste.

Brush some of the paste on the edge of the sides of one of the biscuits. Press it against the edge of one of the sides of the other biscuits. Hold it together for about one minute.

2 Join the biscuit shapes together in this way to make a house. If the house is a bit wobbly, you can use strips of marzipan to hold the walls together.

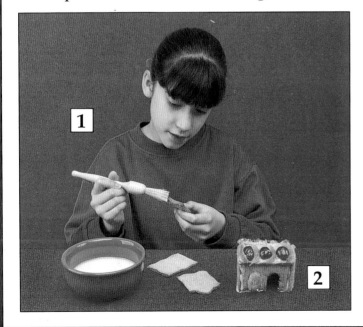

3 There are lots of ways you can decorate your house. Use the icing sugar paste to stick dried fruit and sweets on to the roof.

Try to make a different shaped building, but keep the shapes simple and make sure the pieces fit together.

More things to think about

This book shows you how to make and model salt dough and papier-mâché, how to print paper and dye fabric. You can use these different craft techniques to make your own objects based on food.

To get some ideas for making your own craft objects, think about some of the different kinds of food in the world; how it is grown, prepared, cooked and eaten. Think of the difference between raw and cooked food, or the number of different ways that food, such as eggs or potatoes, can be prepared. Why do you think we eat different kinds of food in the morning, afternoon and evening?

Many cultures use food as a craft medium but it's important to remember that food is for eating. Always ask permission before using any type of food as a craft material. Try to use food as the inspiration for your craft object, rather than making objects from it.

Visit your local art gallery, museum or crafts centre to see how artists have shown food now and in the past. In the sixteenth century an Italian artist called Arcomboldo painted portraits, which were collages of pictures of fruit, vegetables and flowers. Try to find some of Arcomboldo's pictures in the library.

Every country has its own customs and traditions, and many are based on food. Think of all the special meals which are associated with festivals. In many religious festivals, people fast for a time and then feast on specially prepared food. Harvest festival celebrates the growing and reaping of food. It's celebrated in many different ways around the world. Do you take part in any traditions and customs at meal times?

Before you make your craft object, think about the best craft technique to use, for example you could model salt dough or papier-mâché or print or dye fabric. Do you want the finished object to be flat or three-dimensional? Do you want it to have moving parts or hang from the wall? When you have answered these and similar questions, think carefully about the best way of making your craft object and the best materials to use.

Experiment with different kinds of decoration for your craft object. Think about the size, shape and texture of different sorts of food. Can you create similar textures with paper, cloth or by modelling salt dough or papier-mâché?

How to find out more

Information books about food

Pot Luck Jo Lawrie (A&C Black)
Cooking and recipes from medieval times to the nineteenth century.

Breakfast Lisa Chaney (A&C Black)
Photographs, objects and documents show a middle-class breakfast at the turn of the century.

Food for thought Gill Standring (A&C Black)
A book which looks at the environmental effects of factory farming.

* **Science through cookery** Peter Mellet and Jane Rossiter (Franklin Watts)
The science behind cooking.

* **Threads** (A&C Black)
How everyday materials are used and processed, including activities. Relevant titles include **Beans**, **Bread**, **Eggs**, **Fruit**, **Milk**, **Rice**, **Spices**, **Tea** and **Water**.

Fiction

The Marzipan pig Russell Hoban (Puffin)

Magic mash Peter Firmin (A&C Black)

Books about crafts and technology

* **Fresh start** (Franklin Watts)
A step-by-step approach to different craft media. Titles include **Clay**, **Fabric art**, **Papier mâché**, **Masks**, **Paper crafts** and **Jewellery crafts**.

* **Arts and crafts** (Wayland)
A clear step-by-step approach to crafts with ideas for developing designs. Titles include **Batik and tie-dye**, **Block printing** and **Weaving**.

* **Toybox science** Chris Ollerenshaw and Pat Triggs (A&C Black)
Scientific principles explained through toys. A helpful guide to making working models.

* **Make it work** Peter Firmin (A&C Black)

How to build working models from rubbish, including the technology of pulleys, levers and winches.

* indicates a series rather than one book.

Places to visit

The following list gives a selection of places to visit which have major collections of objects from around the world. Don't forget to look in your local town or city museum too.

Commonwealth Institute
230 Kensington High Street, London W8
Each country in the commonwealth has its own display of art and crafts.

Horniman Museum
100 London Road, London SE23
A collection showing arts, crafts and religions of the world.

Pitt Rivers Museum
South Parks Road, Oxford OX1 3PP
Lieutenant General Pitt Rivers, born in 1827, collected a wide range of objects from countries all over the world which he visited as a soldier.

Victoria and Albert Museum
Cromwell Road, London SW7
A vast collection of nineteenth century artefacts.

The Robert Opie Collection of Advertisting and Packaging
Albert Warehouse, Gloucester Docks, Gloucester GL1 2EH

Cogges Manor Farm Museum
Church Lane, Cogges, Witney, Oxon OX8 6LA
Farm kitchens and a dairy of about 1890 set in a working farm. Demonstrations of a kitchen and dairy at work.

A useful address

British Food Information Service, Food from Britain, 5th floor, 524 Market Towers, New Covent Garden Market, London SW8 5NQ

Index

First published 1993
A & C Black (Publishers) Limited
35 Bedford Row, London WC1R 4JH

ISBN 0 7136 3715 3
© 1993 A & C Black (Publishers)
Limited

A CIP catalogue record for this book
is available from the British Library.

Acknowledgements
Line drawings by Barbara Pegg
Photographs by Zul Mukhida, except
for: p12, p18 Life File Photographic
Agency; p22 Format Photographic
Agency; p24 Mexican Ministry of
Tourism.

With grateful thanks to Langford and
Hill Limited, London, for supplying
all art materials.

Craft objects made by Tracy Brunt
except for those on p14–15, p20–21
which were made by Dorothy Moir.

Filmset by Rowland Phototypesetting
Limited, Bury St Edmunds, Suffolk
Printed in England by Cambus Litho